Preparation for Promotion

DR. CONNIE WILLIAMS

Scripture references are noted.

Preparation for Promotion

By: Dr. Connie Williams

Copyright © 2015 Melchizedek Global Publishing
Roswell, Georgia

Printed in the United States of America

Editing: Paula Chambers and Kito Johnson

Cover Design: Kito Johnson

www.MelchizedekGlobal.net

www.DrConnieWilliams.org

ISBN: 069245862X
ISBN-13: 978-0692458624

PREPARATION FOR PROMOTION

.

DR. CONNIE WILLIAMS

DEDICATION

This book is written for and dedicated to those who have experienced challenges in life. To those who at one point or another, whether inwardly or from a mountain top, asked God "Why?!"

DR. CONNIE WILLIAMS

CONTENTS

Foreword

FOREWORD

Have you ever been through some not-so-pleasant

situations? Have you ever questioned, Lord, am I

going to make it? Have you ever thought silently, I

want this all to just be over?

I know; I've been there too.

1
ENOUGH IS ENOUGH

I had a friend in the ministry, and she said, "God, it is enough!" So she wrote a note saying, "I'm dead now. I went willingly. The Father came and got me. This is how I want to be buried. Don't touch me; and don't touch up my makeup!" After writing the note, she put on all her makeup, fixed herself up, laid down on her bed, and said, "Take me God." The result? She fell asleep and took a nap. When she woke up, she was in a fit because she was serious. She was ready to be buried right there. But all she got was a nap. A bit disappointed, she decided, "I guess I might as well just get on up, and see what else God has for me."

Do you know the feeling? Have you wanted to lie down at times and say, "God, just go ahead and take me. It'll be alright. Now I don't want any trauma, and I don't want any drama. But you know I'm in a place of complete despair—a place where I just don't know what's going on. I know it's all good because I know you love me, and I love you. I know I'm going to heaven. I know all that stuff, but..."

You know that place of frustration you walk in sometimes—when you've been through some tough life events. It makes you wonder and ask, why in the world did I have to go through that? And you want answers...ASAP! Now, some might blame the devil, but I'm not sure that I would. The reason why is because... everything that comes into your life has God's handprints on it. It doesn't matter how ugly it looks—nothing comes into your life without God's fingerprint. Nothing comes into your life that God will not turn for the better (Romans 8:28-29). Even those situations that initially look like devastation—God will always find a way to make them into a blessing. Ecclesiastes 3:11 tells us, "He has made all things beautiful in their time." Everything in your life has a beautiful time. If it's not beautiful, it's just because the time hasn't come. It could be a job loss, a divorce, even death; He has made all—ALL—things beautiful in its time. So if you have something ugly in your life that you are going through, or that you have been through, hold on to God's promise. Know that before God is finished, that ugliness will become something beautiful; and you will testify to the fact that, had it not been for that nasty thing, you would not be who you are right now.

2
AN UGLY TESTIMONY

I find something good in everything. I minister to prostitutes, inmates, and drug addicts and dealers alike. I have a driver that takes care of me whenever I go to this particular church. On one occasion, when I was visiting this church, God told me that the driver had been to prison for murder.

I said (hesitantly), "Brother? You ever, uh,

you ever been to prison?"

He said, "Yeah."

I asked, "What for? Murder?"

"Yeah," he replied.

So, I said, "Now, this doesn't matter to me, but God's telling me that you killed eight people."

He said, "That's right. I tried to kill a ninth, but he just wouldn't lie down."

I responded, "Have I told you how much I love you today? That doesn't even count when you picked me up yesterday. Did I tell you I love you TODAY?!" We both laughed.

God shared that with me because that

young man was still carrying the weight of his past. My friend, there are things that happen in our lives that are downright ugly, nasty, perhaps embarrassing, but God has a plan for it.

I have a friend named Lola who lived life as a prostitute for a time, now she ministers to the prostitutes. I have another friend that has probably never said a foul word, never smoked cigarette, never had a drink of liquor, or anything like that. When I found that out, I said, "Girl, you don't know what you missed. It's too late for you now. You should've tried it before you got saved." Now I can only speak for myself, but I enjoyed every drink I ever had—especially Wild Turkey. If it had Wild Turkey in it, I'd drink it. I enjoyed every drink I ever drank in my life. If God had not interrupted my life, my life would look very different today. You wouldn't find me at church on any given Sunday morning because I would be sleeping off a hangover.

I have heard people say, "softly and tenderly Jesus is calling," and I'm sure He is; but my reality is that He didn't softly and tenderly call me. He jumped right in and interrupted my life; and when He did, I said, "Wait a minute, this is not a good time for me." I mean I had a party to go to the next weekend. Seriously, I tried to negotiate with God. I told Him I would go to church after the party—maybe not Sunday morning, but definitely Sunday night.

Have you ever tried to negotiate with God? How did that work out for you?

Here's the truth... Every "not so smart" thing you have done, every trial you have been through, every mistake you have made... I promise you that God has made, or will make, something out of it. Do you remember the account in Matthew 14 of the feeding of the 5,000?

> "And he commanded the multitude to sit down on the grass, and took the five loaves, and the two fishes, and looking up to heaven, he blessed, and brake, and gave the loaves to his

disciples, and the disciples to the multitude. And they did all eat, and were filled: and they took up of the fragments that remained twelve baskets full. And they that had eaten were about five thousand men, beside women and children."

(Matthew 14:19-21 KJV)

Jesus fed the multitudes with only two fish and five loaves of bread. Many times we think that is the miracle. Granted, it is quite miraculous; but just as miraculous were the twelve baskets of leftover bread collected after the meal. If Jesus started out with a couple of fish and a few loaves of bread, yet He paid careful attention to take up the twelve baskets of scraps, then we can be assured that it is God's pattern to make great use of scraps. That includes making great use of the scraps in our lives... yours included!

So be sure that for every challenge you have faced in your life, you have not suffered in vain. The friend I mentioned earlier (the one that had never uttered a foul word) said to me, "I'm going to go down the street and help Lola. She's going to minister to the prostitutes, and I'm going with her."

I replied, "You better just go on to your Sunday school class because, when you go down in the streets with those women, they are not going to be impressed with bible tracts and Sunday school pens. They are going to take those pens and beat you to death with them. Now you let Lola go on down there because she knows how to minister to them. Those women aren't going to be impressed with you. You will come back with those Sunday school pens stuck in your head."

Who is a prostitute going to listen to? The prostitute doesn't care about someone with a cute little Sunday school lesson. She is fighting for her life. Who else but Lola could go minister to those ladies? Someone that's been through something of a similar nature! I am simply saying that your ugly testimony "qualifies you" for ministry.

3
IT'S JUST LIFE

I know what it's like to say, I'm saved and baptized in the Holy Ghost. I go to church and do everything that I know to do; and yet, I have been walking through hell. Perhaps you feel like God is not cutting you any slack, and you're getting hit from every side. Let me suggest that what you are going through may not be by the hand of God or by the hand of the devil… it may just be "life."

I believe God can be found somewhere in all things but I have also discovered, after a myriad of experiences, there is a reality called "life." And some things shouldn't be blamed on God, nor should they be blamed on the devil. Someone once called me and said, "The devil tore up my washing machine."

I said, "Honey, isn't that the machine that your momma used to have?" She replied, "Yes it is." I chuckled and said, "No, it's not the devil… your washing machine is just old." That's life.

Another might say, "This boy broke my heart." Again, that is just life.

Some stuff is just life. There is a comfort that comes with knowing that regardless of what happens, whatever life brings your way... ultimately, God will make it profitable. Just as Joseph eventually realized concerning his brothers cruel treatment of him; God will turn it for you and He will use it to take you to a higher place. Somehow, some way.

> "But as for you, ye thought evil against me; but God meant it unto good, to bring to pass, as it is this day, to save much people alive."
>
> (Genesis 50:20 KJV)

DR. CONNIE WILLIAMS

4

WHEN RIGHT FEELS WRONG

When you are going through uncomfortable moments, have you ever thought that you must have done something wrong or that you had missed God in some way? Perhaps you are wondering right now what you have possibly done to be where you are right now.

Could it be... that maybe you didn't do

anything wrong (other than the stupid stuff we all do)? Could it be... that maybe you did something right? You have been struggling and thinking that you are in tribulation. Could it be... that it is not tribulation at all? It is true: In the earthly world you face tribulation. But are you really in the world? The truth is, as a believer, you are here on this earth; but you are not of this world. Your citizenship is from above. So, could it be that you are going through a tough time because you have done something right?

But, why? What sense does that make? It is good to remember that God sees and knows your heart, and God sees potential inside of you that you may not see yourself. In order to draw out that potential, in order to move you closer to perfection in love, God has to cut some of the raw edges off. It can be painful when He chooses to cut some of the scraggly branches off. Sometimes He cuts some relationships off—those that are not profitable to you. And it is not because He is mad at you; but it is because He sees something greater to be revealed in you.

> "I am the true vine, and my Father is the husbandman. Every branch in me that beareth not fruit he taketh away: and every branch that beareth fruit, he purgeth it, that it may bring forth more

fruit. Now ye are clean

through the word which I

have spoken unto you."

(John 15:1-3 KJV)

In this passage, Jesus is talking to a people that already have relationship with the Word. He is not talking to backsliders or the unsaved or the multitudes... He is saying, 'I am talking to you that have already heard the Word, to you that are already clean, to you that already love God, to you that are already a part of the body of Christ... You are the ones I am talking to.'

Jesus continues...

Abide in me, and I in you. As

the branch cannot bear fruit

of itself, except it abide in the vine; no more can ye, except ye abide in me. I am the vine, ye are the branches: He that abideth in me, and I in him, the same bringeth forth much fruit: for without me ye can do nothing. If a man abide not in me, he is cast forth as a branch, and is withered; and men gather them, and cast them into the fire, and they are burned. If ye abide in me, and my words abide in you, ye shall ask what ye will, and it shall be done unto you. Herein is my Father glorified, that ye bear much fruit; so shall ye be my disciples. (John 15:4-8 KJV)

What Jesus says here—about the vine and the branches—is not only deep, but critical for you to understand as a Christian. Again...He says, if you bear fruit, then I am going to purge you. I am going to cut you. I am going to prune you. If you bear fruit... This really doesn't seem right, does it? If you are bearing fruit, you ought to get a car or something, right? Yes, be rewarded with a car, a new house, or at least a new outfit, if you are already bearing fruit for God. But, no—instead, you are going to get cut.

Has God seen fruit in your life?

Even if you are thinking, 'No, not me, I don't have any fruit.' I imagine He has seen you bear more fruit in your life than you would ever guess. Even if you are not sure about the 'bearing fruit' thing... one thing I can tell you with total certainty, is that God has seen (and sees) potential in you that you aren't even aware of yet. And because of that fruit (be it known or unknown to you) and your potential, God has been—and is— purging you. Maybe you are thinking... "I've done just fine during my life and I don't want any part of that purging or fruit stuff. I don't want to bear fruit: I don't want to be purged: I don't need it. "

Well, God saw (and sees) something in your heart—whether you choose to acknowledge it or not. For this reason, there is a purging taking place that you do not have the power to stop. And why would you want to? God sees much more in you than you will ever see! In fact, He said, "ye have not chosen me, but I have chosen you" (John 15:16a KJV).

5
BEYOND THE FRUIT... NO LIMITS!

God has seen something in your life that bears witness of Him. What have other people been witnessing of your behavior lately? Might it be less than Christ-like? Aren't we blessed that God doesn't see our potential based upon our behavior? Instead, God looks on the heart. In reality, 'luck' has nothing to do with it, for it is purely by God's grace that He chooses to look within—rather than without.

Whatever you have been through, or are going through, or will go through, here is some advice to keep in mind. You are not in the midst of tribulation. You are not in the midst of an attack by the devil. And God is not mad at you. Simply put, God has seen something in your life called fruit. God has seen something good in you. And, as I said earlier, though you may be expecting a 'blessing' as 'payment' for those fruits, God often says... 'Wait a minute. Don't limit me to a house or a car when I've got a plan to give you true wealth of much higher value!'

Now true enough, there are some

intangible rewards that come from bearing fruit. Perhaps you helped a person in need, taught a children's Sunday school class, or served in some other meaningful way and you left feeling satisfied or fulfilled knowing that you made a difference in someone's life. There is nothing wrong with this type of self-satisfaction—or self-reward—as long as you don't let it go to your head. Be careful not to feed your ego to the point that you forget that it is your connection with the Father through Jesus that you possess the power for fruit to be born through your life (John 15:5).

While a sense of self-satisfaction is a human reaction to fruit, God's reaction is different. When God sees fruit, God sees potential in your life.

When God sees potential, He says... "Wait a minute. Let me 'groom' that up a little bit. Let me shave that off a little bit. Let me change that thought pattern a little bit. Let me change the language in your vocabulary a little bit. Let me change your vision and how you look at things a little bit." When God sees fruit in your life, He 'rewards' you with a purging—a cutting away—and a downsizing for the purposes of, 1) not carrying dead branches into your next day, and 2) growth. When you prune a tree, you give it a serious cutting. There have been times I've pruned in my garden and afterwards, I look at a poor stump and think, "I bet I killed it. It is not going to come back from this. Or, if it does manage to survive, it is going to be pretty unattractive." But when spring rolls around and that tree does grow, it is bigger and more beautiful than it ever was. God prunes you in order to take you to a higher place—to transform you.

DR. CONNIE WILLIAMS

6
PREPARATION FOR PROMOTION

If you ever feel like you have missed God, or that you have done something wrong because nothing is going right... Stop! Turn that thinking around. You must have done something right! Not everybody is pruned or purged. Everybody goes through tough times, but pruning is for potential. Purging is for promotion. Although it rarely feels that way. Purging can be painful, sometimes even bloody. Sometimes God will cut us back until we feel like there isn't anything left. But know that God is preparing you for a promotion that you could not handle if those dead branches were still in the way. God sliced them off in order for you to bear more fruit… greater fruit that remains.

As you are purged and come into your new place in God—a new realm—you can't carry everything with you. You can't carry negative thoughts in you. You can't carry negative speech or gossip with you. You can't carry hatred or bitterness or strife. You can't afford to carry anything toxic with you. It has all got to be cut away. It is painful but it is preparation. Know that, because God has seen something inside of you, He has to do a little refining—a little tweaking, here and there.   And when God does that, He causes you to bloom in greater ways than you have ever seen before.

So go forth today with the assurance that God, who is the gardener of your life, knows your heart and He knows that you love Him. Remember that He abides in you and He sees potential in you. Remember that God, who makes all things beautiful, brings good out of every disappointment and trial in your life. Remember that God, who purges for promotion, is consistently refining you in order to take you farther and higher and greater than you could imagine.

.

ABOUT THE AUTHOR

Dr. Connie Williams is a renowned international author, teacher and prophetic voice. Known for her creative apostolic flow, she graces this age with a new dimension of revelatory knowledge in scripture, mysteries, patterns and cycles. Her ministry has served as major breakthroughs for the church, world affairs, corporate business and the entertainment industry.

After over 30 years of carrying the Gospel of Christ and experiencing great personal revelation,

Dr. Williams's ministry took a certain shift in 2012. Though she's always been known to transcend religious and cultural boundaries with the unconditional love of God, Dr. Williams now travels extensively releasing the Word of the Lord concerning the King-Priest Order of Melchizedek. From this eternal order the manifested sons of God are being revealed in the earth to answer the groan of creation.

To learn more, visit:

www.DrConnieWilliams.org

PREPARATION FOR PROMOTION

DR. CONNIE WILLIAMS